The Best of The MAILBOX Magazine

Early Literacy

The best early literacy activities from the 2004–2009 issues of *The Mailbox®* magazine

- ● Circle-time activities
- ● Small-group activities
- ● Games
- ● Center activities

- ● Thematic units
- ● Songs, rhymes, & poems
- ● Full-color cards
- ● Patterns

Managing Editor: Brenda Fay

Editorial Team: Becky S. Andrews, Diane Badden, Kimberley Bruck, Karen A. Brudnak, Pam Crane, Chris Curry, Pierce Foster, Tazmen Hansen, Marsha Heim, Lori Z. Henry, Sheila Krill, Debra Liverman, Kitty Lowrance, Mark Rainey, Greg D. Rieves, Hope Rodgers-Medina, Rebecca Saunders, Donna K. Teal, Sharon M. Tresino, Zane Williard

www.themailbox.com

Table of Contents

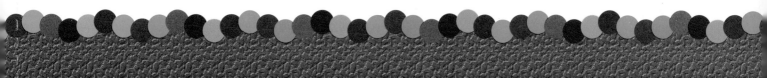

Circle Time

Circle Time

Watermelon Rhymes

There's a delicious outcome to this rhyming activity! Cut out the rhyming cards on page 13 and attach each one to a construction paper seed cutout. Spread a picnic cloth on the floor and gather youngsters on it. Enlist your students' help in identifying the picture on each seed; then hand out the seeds. Tell students that every seed rhymes with another seed. Give students a few minutes to make the rhyming matches on their own. Then provide assistance as needed. Place each pair of rhyming seeds on a different paper plate. Celebrate your students' efforts with a snack of real watermelon!

Suzanne Maxymuk
Evergreen School
Woodbury, NJ

Picture Poem

This engaging poem helps youngsters develop rhyming skills! In advance, cut out the picture cards on page 11. Attach the cards to a wall in the order shown. Then recite the poem with your youngsters, pointing to each card to help youngsters supply the rhyming words.

I'm a gray bat; I'm a gray bat.
What rhymes with *bat*? *Hat*!
I'm a monster's hat; I'm a monster's hat.
What rhymes with *hat*? *Cat*!
I'm a brown cat; I'm a brown cat.
What rhymes with *cat*? *Rat*!
I'm a squeaky rat; I'm a squeaky rat,
And that is that!

Bonnie C. Krum
St. Matthew's Early Education Center
Bowie, MD

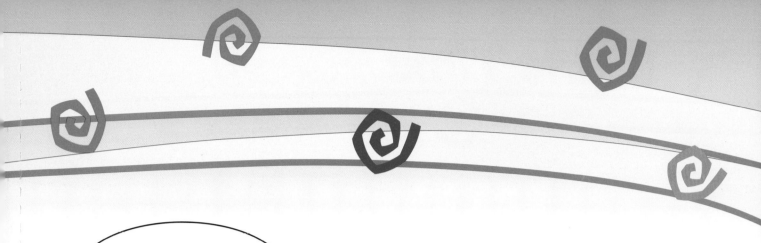

That's not a norse! It's a horse!

Trouble on the Farm

Youngsters develop phonological awareness with this adorable idea! Cut out the farm animal cards on pages 15 and 17 and place them in a bag. Then don a straw hat and a bandana and introduce yourself as the farmer. Explain that you have had some trouble with the animals not answering your call. Next, remove a card from the bag and say the animal's name, replacing the initial consonant. No doubt youngsters will immediately correct your error. Continue in the same way with each animal card.

Gail Marsh, Pacific, MO

Hatching Sounds

Youngsters pretend to be ducks during this fun phonological awareness activity. In advance, cut out a copy of the picture cards on page 19 and attach each card to a separate egg cutout. Invite several youngsters to each sit on a different egg. Choose a child and say the rhyme shown. Then have the child hop off her egg and name the picture on it. Help her identify whether the name of the picture begins with the /d/ sound. Then collect her egg. Continue with the remaining youngsters. Then repeat the activity with other students and different eggs.

Hop off your egg with a quack, quack, quack,
And tell us all what picture you see.
Does it begin with /d/, /d/, /d/
Or something other than letter *D*?

Ada Goren, Winston-Salem, NC

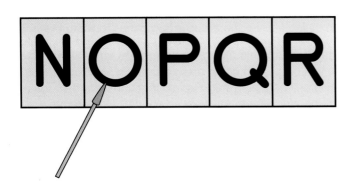

Getting Warmer!

This letter-recognition activity is sure to cause lots of giggles! Gather youngsters around your alphabet display. Choose a letter, such as *P*, and point to a letter near letter *P* on the display. Ask youngsters whether the letter you're pointing to is *P*. After students confirm that the letter is not *P*, point to another letter nearby and ask students whether you are getting warmer (closer to the letter *P*) or colder (farther away from the letter *P*). Continue in the same way until youngsters lead you to the correct letter. There it is!

Linda Bille
Riviera United Methodist Preschool
Redondo Beach, CA

Letter Search

For this letter recognition activity, write each student's name on a card and place the cards in a bag. Also write a desired letter on a sheet of chart paper. To begin, invite a volunteer to remove a card from the bag. Identify the name on the card and have the volunteer give it to its owner. Help the child decide whether the letter shown is found in her name. If it is, add her name to the page, writing the target letter in a different color. If her name does not have the letter, have her place the card in a discard pile and remove a new card from the bag. Continue in this manner for several rounds. Play this game many times throughout the school year, choosing a different letter each time!

Jennifer Schear
Clover Patch Preschool
Cedar Falls, IA

Doggie, Doggie

To prepare for this letter-identification game, label a class supply of dog-bone cutouts (pattern on page 64) with different letters. Invite a volunteer to pretend to be a napping dog. Give each remaining child in the group a dog bone. To wake the doggie, chant, "Doggie, where's the bone with the *B*? Someone has it, but it isn't me!" The doggie picks one of the children, who then holds up her bone and identifies the letter. Play continues until the doggie picks the child with the correct bone; then she becomes the doggie. When she is "asleep," have students exchange bones with classmates. Then play another round!

Leigh Ann Peter, Buttonwood Preschool, Lumberton, NJ

Delivering Letters

Youngsters pretend to be mail carriers in this fun letter-identification activity! Put a different letter card in each of several envelopes; then place the envelopes in a tote bag. Give the bag to a volunteer and ask her to pretend she is a mail carrier. Next, play a recording of music and have the mail carrier walk around the outside of the circle. When you stop the music, instruct her to hand an envelope to a classmate. Have the recipient remove the card from the envelope and hold it in the air; then have the class identify the letter. Finally, have the two students switch places. Repeat the process until all the mail has been delivered.

Circle Time

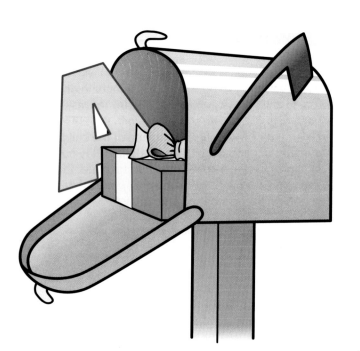

Letters in the Mail

Preschoolers love to get mail, so try this special delivery idea that builds letter-sound association skills! Place a real mailbox in your classroom. Each week, place a die-cut version of the letter you'll be studying inside the mailbox for youngsters to discover. Also add a package with a letter-related surprise, such as acorns for the letter *A* or Band-Aid strips for the letter *B*. Hey—we've got mail!

Nancy Foss
Wee Care
Galion, OH

Peck a Letter

Little ones practice letter-sound association with this fun activity! Program several craft foam seed cutouts with different letters. Obtain a bird puppet or stuffed bird toy. To begin, scatter the birdseed faceup on the floor. Then invite a student to "fly" the bird around the circle as you recite the chant shown. After you make the letter sound, the child gently swoops the bird to the floor and uses it to peck the seed with the corresponding letter. Then have her pass the bird to a classmate. Continue as time allows.

Little birdie, fly to the ground
And peck the letter that makes the sound [/s/].

Donna Brock
High Desert Montessori Child Care Center
Hesperia, CA

Up and Down Letters

To prepare for this activity, gather a supply of uppercase and lowercase letter cards. Have youngsters sit in your large-group area. Then show them a card. If the card shows an uppercase letter, have the students stand up. If it shows a lowercase letter, encourage them to stay seated. Once youngsters have decided whether the letter is uppercase or lowercase, help them name the letter. Then have them stay in the same position and repeat the process with another card. What an active letter review!

Paula Diekhoff
Head Start
Warsaw, IN

That's an uppercase letter!

Searching for Shells

Review uppercase- and lowercase-letter recognition with a seashell hunt right in the classroom! Program shell cutouts (pattern on page 21) with either the uppercase or lowercase form of a familiar letter. Hide the shells around the classroom. During group time, have students search for shells. When every child has found one or more, gather the class in the group area. Then help the children sort the letters—uppercase into one sand pail and lowercase into another. Keep the pails handy in case additional shells are located! Plan to repeat the activity using different letters.

Amy Aloi
Bollman Bridge RECC
Jessup, MD

Circle Time

Elephant Pointers

Little ones take a look at words and letters with this simple and engaging picture book! In advance, make an elephant pointer similar to the one shown (pattern on page 21). Read aloud the story *Elephants Aloft* by Kathi Appelt, pausing occasionally to have students study a chosen word. Invite a child to use the elephant pointer to point to the first letter in the word and the last letter in the word. Also invite students to point to and identify any familiar letters they see. If desired, follow up the book reading by having each youngster make his own elephant pointer. Place the pointers in a center; then encourage visiting children to practice pointing to the first and last letters of words they see around the room. No doubt this activity will be a humongous hit!

Rainy-Day Poem

With this activity, students develop an awareness of words as separate units of print. Make a class supply of the poem on page 22. Have each child attach a raindrop sticker or cutout to a craft stick to make a minipointer. (Be sure to make a copy of the poem and a pointer for yourself!) Display the page and have youngsters watch as you read the poem aloud, pointing to each word with your pointer. Then give each child his paper and pointer. Read each line aloud, encouraging little ones to follow along and point to each word as you read.

adapted from an idea by Louise Frankel
Family Development Day Care, Plainfield, NJ

Spring Rain

Splish, splash,
Drip, drop!
Raindrops fall,
Plip, plop.
Falling faster,
Raindrops race.
Tickle, tickle
On my face!

adapted from a poem by Nancy C. Allen
Ashley Abbey Learning Center
Mechanicsville, VA

TEC61327

TEC61327

TEC61327

TEC61327

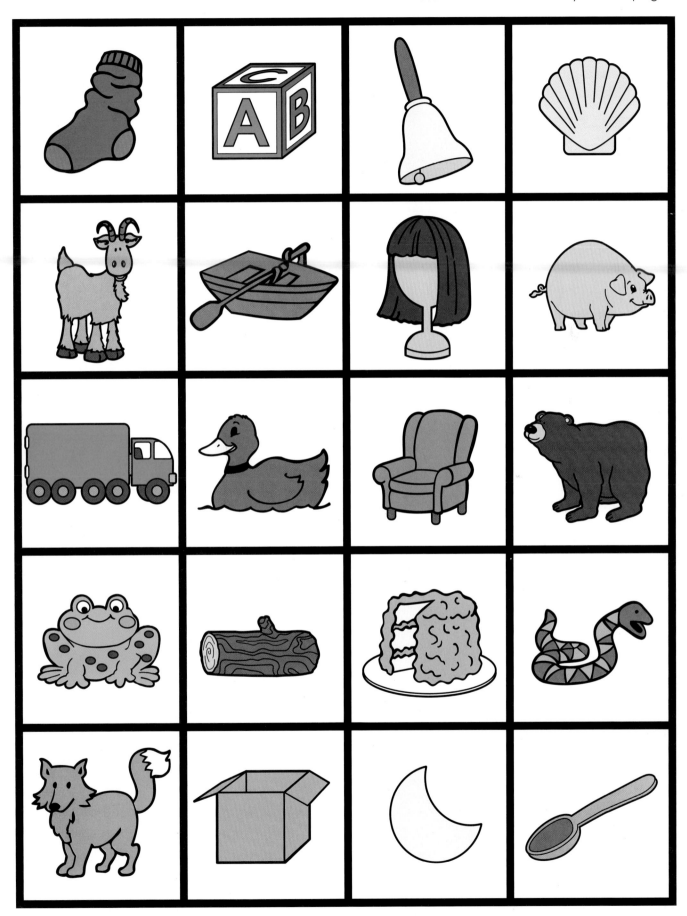

TEC61327

TEC61327

TEC61327

TEC61327

16

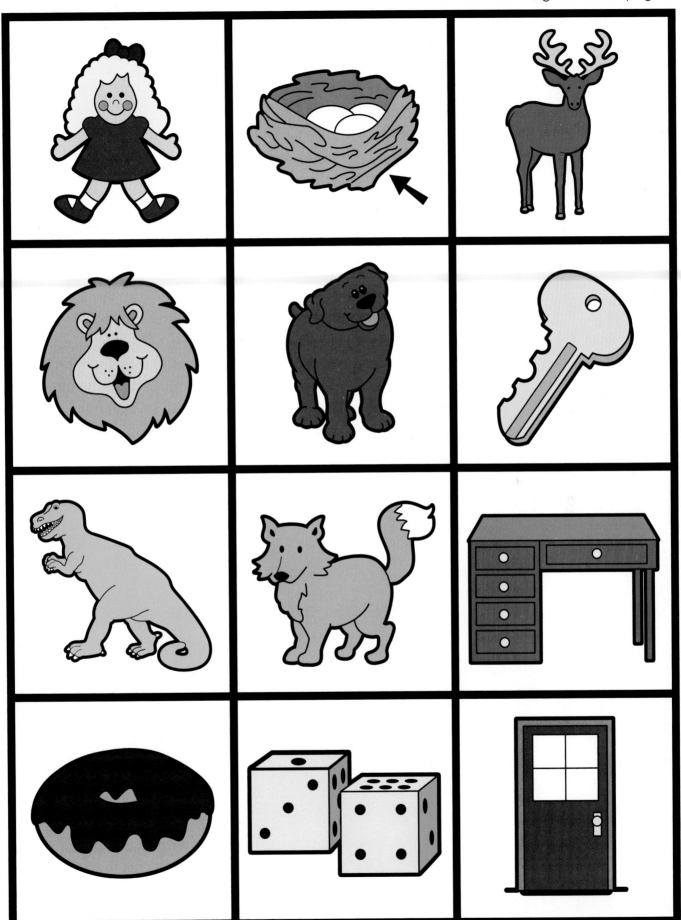

Shell Pattern
Use with "Searching for Shells" on page 9.

TEC61327

Elephant Pattern
Use with "Elephant Pointers" on page 10.

TEC61327

Spring Rain

Splish, splash,

Drip, drop!

Raindrops fall,

Plip, plop.

Falling faster,

Raindrops race.

Tickle, tickle

On my face!

adapted from a poem by Nancy C. Allen
Ashley Abbey Learning Center
Mechanicsville, VA

Note to the teacher: Use with "Rainy-Day Poem" on page 10.

Learning Centers

Learning Centers

A Dinosaur Dig
Recognizing one's name

With this name recognition idea, your little archaeologists dig for their very own personalized dinosaurs! Make a class supply of dinosaur cutouts (patterns on page 30). Label each cutout with a different child's name. Laminate the dinosaurs; then bury them in your sand table. A visiting youngster digs through the sand to find the dinosaur with his name. Then he places it back in the sand for future digging adventures!

Sue Reppert
Widening World Preschool
Mentor, OH

Under the Sea—I See Me!
Recognizing classmates' names

Bolster little ones' name recognition with this fun sensory idea! Write each child's name on a plain index card. Then use clear Con-Tact covering to adhere the names to the bottom of your empty water table. Fill the table with plain or blue-tinted water before inviting youngsters to look for their own names and the names of their classmates as they explore this center. What a splash!

Dawn Michelle Schu
Chicago, IL

Letters in My Name
Recognizing letters in one's name

Focus on letter sorting with this delicious activity! To prepare, create a simple T chart like the one shown and then make a class supply. Place the charts at your literacy center, along with a plastic bag of Alpha-Bits cereal for each child and sentence strips with children's names. Have a child find his name strip and then refer to it as he sorts the cereal letters onto the chart. After all his cereal pieces have been sorted, invite him to eat all the letters for a yummy snack!

Catherine Brubaker, Girard Head Start, Coldwater, MI

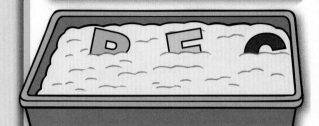

Diggin' for Letters
Matching letters

Stash some letters in your sand table for a center that's a real treasure! To prepare, make two sets of letter cutouts. Glue one set of letters to a length of paper as shown; then attach the hook side of a Velcro fastener to each letter. Display the paper near your sand table. Attach the corresponding loop sides of Velcro fasteners to each letter in the remaining set. Bury the loose letter cutouts in your sand table. A youngster removes a letter from the sand and then attaches it to the matching letter on the display. He continues in the same way with other letters he finds in the sand.

Beth Edwards, Wintergreen Primary School
Greenville, NC

CD Clip
Matching letters

Glue construction paper circles to recycled compact discs; then label each circle with a different letter. Program a supply of spring-style clothespins with letters that correspond to the discs. Place the discs and the clothespins at a center. A child visits the center and clips the clothespins to the matching discs.

Deborah Provencher
West Brookfield Elementary
West Brookfield, MA

Letter and Number Lights
Sorting letters and numbers

Make a supply of lightbulb cutouts (patterns on page 31). Label half the bulbs with different letters and the remaining half with different numbers. Attach two separate lengths of yarn to a wall as shown; then attach a letter bulb to one length and a number bulb to the second length. Place the bulbs and a container of spring-style clothespins nearby. A child clips each bulb to the appropriate length.

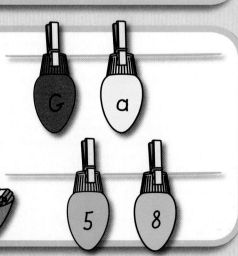

Mary Robles, Milwaukie, OR

Learning Centers

P Is for *Pumpkin!*
Letter-sound association

To prepare, mix pumpkin spice into a batch of orange play dough. Put the play dough at a center along with rolling pins, small pie tins, and several letter *P* cookie cutters. A child visits the center and uses a rolling pin and play dough to make a pretend pie. She uses a cookie cutter to stamp the letter *P* on top of her pie. Then she identifies the letter name and its sound.

Jennifer Nelson
Lindon Elementary
Lindon, UT

Alphabet Hats
Matching letters and sounds

Review letter sounds at a center that's filled with fashion! First, duplicate the hat and flower patterns on page 32 onto tagboard, making one set for each letter you wish to review. Color the hats and flowers as desired and cut them out. Label each flower with a letter and glue onto each hat a picture of an item whose name has a corresponding beginning sound. Put the hats and flowers in your literacy center and have youngsters practice matching letters to their beginning sounds.

Suzanne Maxymuk, Evergreen Avenue School
Woodbury, NJ

It Begins With a...
Matching letters and sounds

Review letter sounds with this interactive bulletin board. To begin, post several die-cut letters in no particular order on a bulletin board or wall space within youngsters' reach. Add three or four pieces of the hook side of self-adhesive Velcro fastener near each letter. Then cut out three or four magazine pictures or pictures of clip art for each letter. Add the loop side of the Velcro fastener to each picture. Then put all the pictures in a bag near the board.

A child at this center pulls a picture from the bag, decides which letter it begins with, and attaches it near that letter. *S* is for *sun!*

Leigh Ann Peter, Buttonwood Preschool, Lumberton, NJ

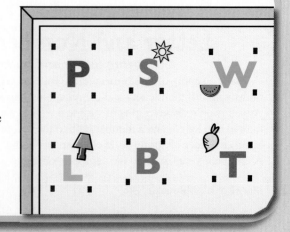

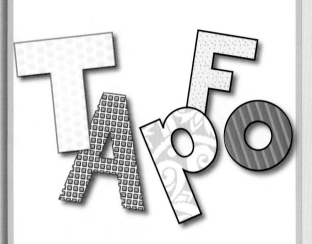

Textured Letters
Developing letter formation awareness

Getting a feel for letters is what this literacy center is all about! Cut several alphabet letters from tagboard. Then cut the same set of letters from a variety of textured materials, such as sandpaper, felt, upholstery fabric, wallpaper, and bubble wrap. Glue each textured cutout atop its matching tagboard cutout. Little ones will have a grand time feeling the letters and their shapes.

Melanie Hays
Crossgates Methodist Children's Center
Pearl, MS

Shapely Letters
Forming letters

Students form letters with this tactile idea! Write the letter *R* twice on a sheet of poster board as shown. Glue a length of rope to the *R* on the left. Then place the poster board at a center, along with a piece of rope identical to the first piece. Before students visit the center, encourage them to say the word *rope*, emphasizing the /r/ sound. Then have a student visit the center and run his hands over the rope. Encourage him to form the loose rope over the second *R* so it resembles the first. Make other centers similar to this one by using lace for the letter *L*, yarn for the letter *Y*, and string for the letter *S*.

Dot Stein, Christian Beginnings Preschool, Prince Frederick, MD

Letter Building
Forming letters

Little ones can count on loads of letter-formation practice at this center! Place a container of blocks or other large manipulatives in your literacy center, along with a set of oversize letter cards. A child chooses a letter card; then she forms the letter by laying blocks on the card as shown. After she covers the entire letter, encourage her to use more blocks to re-create the letter beside the card.

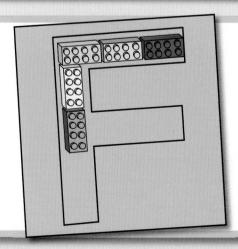

Learning Centers

Letter Rubbings
Developing prewriting skills

Miscellaneous bulletin board letters will be put to good use with this idea! Simply tape several different letters to a table in a center. Provide a supply of light-colored paper and several unwrapped crayons. A youngster visits the center and names one of the letters. After he places a sheet of paper on top of the letter, he rubs the side of a crayon across the paper to reveal the letter underneath.

Brooke Beverly, Dudley Elementary, Dudley, MA

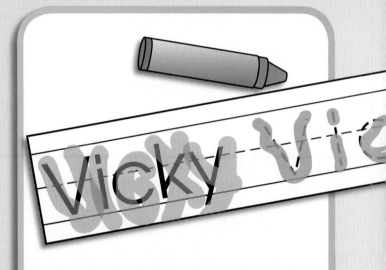

Names, Names, Names
Tracing, writing one's name

These nifty name strips give preschoolers independent practice writing their names! To make each child's name strip, write her name at the left end of a sentence strip and use dotted letters to write her name at the right end of the strip. Laminate the name strips. Then put the strips and wipe-off markers in your writing center. A child finds her name strip and traces each set of letters. After students have practiced writing their names in this way, make a second set of name strips that show dotted letters to the left and no letters to the right. Write on!

Victoria DeOrnellis, Aberdeen Elementary, Aberdeen, MS

Grocery Lists
Tracing words, prewriting

Cut out pictures from grocery store circulars and attach each one to a paper strip. Write the name of each item next to its picture. Then laminate the strips for durability. Also laminate a supply of blank strips. Place the strips at a center and provide access to wipe-off markers. Youngsters visit the center and use the markers to trace the words or to write items of their choosing on the blank strips.

Christine Wirt
Tiny Tot Station
Elk Grove, CA

Calendar Crazy
Writing letters and numbers

Why not put used calendars in your writing area to help preschoolers practice writing letters and numbers? Collect a supply of old calendars and place them at your writing center. Invite children to trace over the letters and numbers on larger calendars or to reproduce each number in the box for that date. After lots of practice writing, print off some blank calendar grids from your computer and invite youngsters to fill in all the numbers and name for the current month. Pretty soon they'll be making whole calendars!

Kaylene Killebrew
Tuscola, IL

I went to my friend's 🏠. She gave me a ⊙ and a 🎂. We went to play.

Rubber Stamp Rebus Stories
Dictating a story

Inspire your young writers to create new stories with the help of some rubber stamps! Gather a collection of interesting stamps to put in your writing center. Have a child choose a few stamps around which he can build a story. Then have an adult helper write as a child dictates a story, letting the child fill in some of the key words by stamping the images on the paper. Invite the authors to share their stories with the class at group time!

Jennifer Schear
Clover Patch Preschool
Cedar Falls, IA

Square by Square
Developing prereading skills

To begin, make a mat by writing words on a large sheet of construction paper, enclosing each letter in a box as shown. Label each word with a corresponding picture. Then cut and label matching letter tiles. Put the letter tiles in a resealable plastic bag and place the bag at a center along with the mat. A child visits the center and matches the letter tiles to the letters on the mat. Once the words are complete, have him look at the pictures to identify each word.

Karen E. McMillan, Pima Community College Child Development Center
Tucson, AZ

Dinosaur Patterns
Use with "A Dinosaur Dig" on page 24.

The Best of The Mailbox® *Early Literacy* • ©The Mailbox® Books • TEC61327

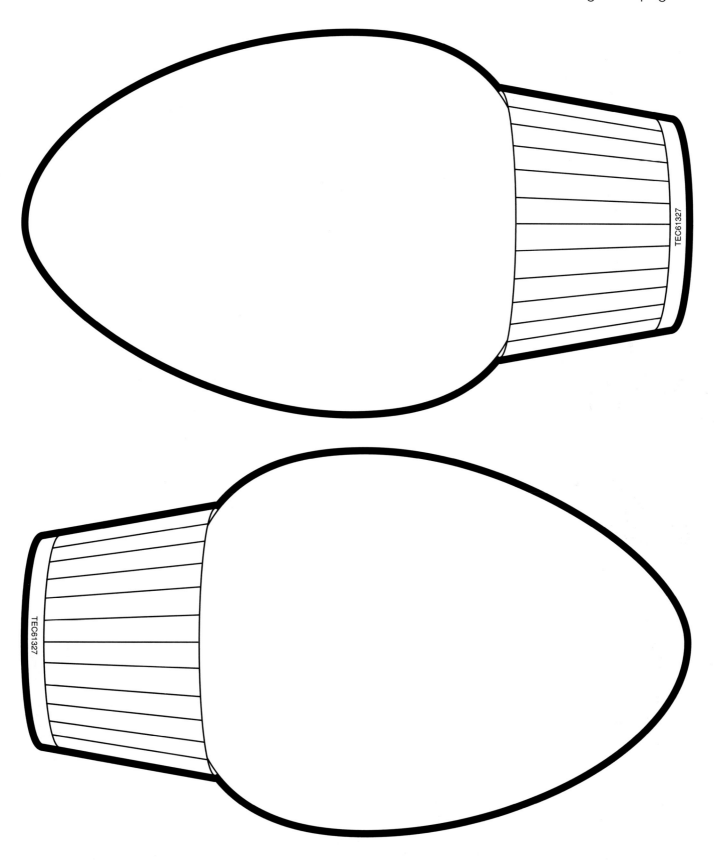

TEC61327

TEC61327

Hat and Flower Patterns
Use with "Alphabet Hats" on page 26.

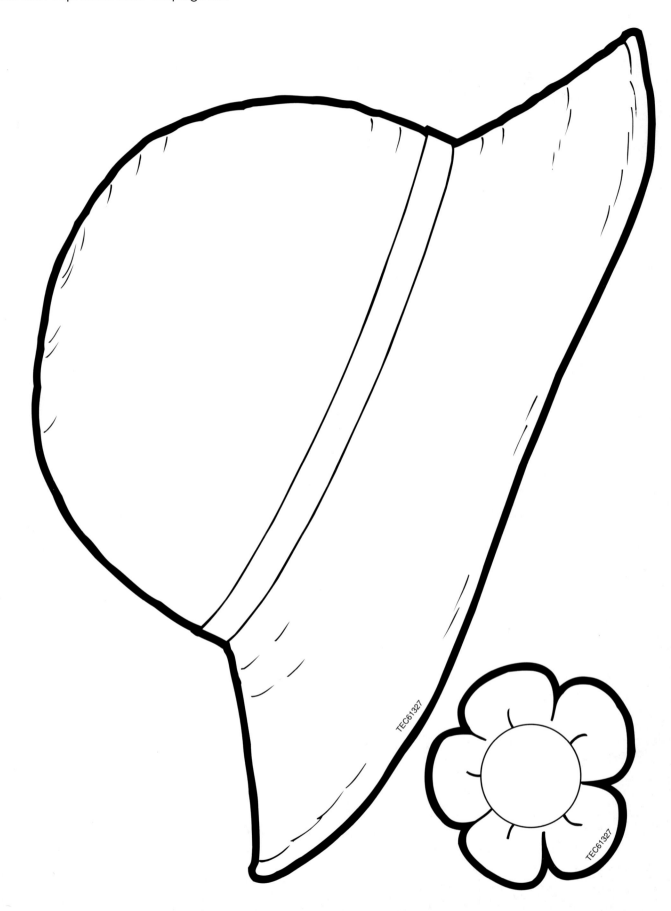

The Best of The Mailbox® *Early Literacy* • ©The Mailbox® Books • TEC61327

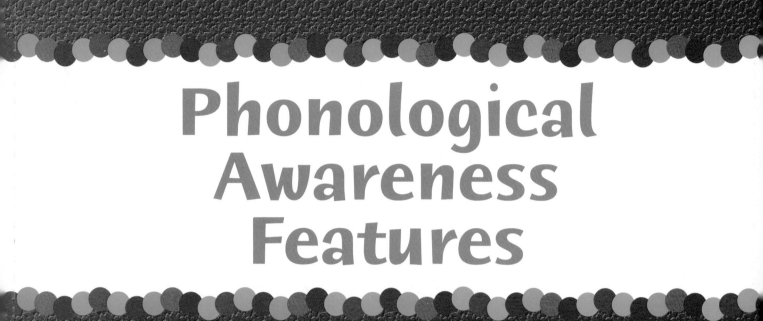

Phonological
Awareness
Features

A "Purr-fect" Time for Rhyme!

Youngsters can sink their paws into these engaging activities, which are perfectly groomed to help them gain an understanding of rhyme!

ideas contributed by Angie Kutzer, Garrett Elementary, Mebane, NC

From Lap to Lap

Bat, hat, mat, sat—there sure are a lot of words that rhyme with *cat*! That's why they're the focus of this nifty whole-group activity! Obtain a small toy stuffed cat or a cat cutout. Gather youngsters in a circle. Chant, "Cat, mat," encouraging students to join you as they pass the cat around the circle. Then say a different rhyme for students to chant, such as "Cat, hat." Continue this rhyming game as long as desired, with students passing the cat from lap to lap all the while. Rhyming words are fun to say!

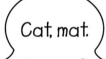

Cat, mat.

Kitty Characteristics

Rhyming words abound in this cute-as-a-button action rhyme! Lead youngsters in performing the rhyme shown, stressing the rhyming word at the end of each line. After repeated performances, drop out before the end of each line and encourage the students to supply the rhyming word.

What do kittens like to do?

They like to nap	*Pretend to sleep.*
On someone's lap.	*Pat your lap.*
They sharpen claws	*Hold up both hands as if they have claws.*
On their front paws.	*Pretend to sharpen claws.*
They like to stalk	*Crouch down like a kitten.*
Where people walk.	*Pretend to stalk.*
They pounce on feet,	*Pounce!*
Then look so sweet.	*Smile sweetly.*

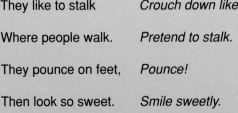

A Hat for a Cat

Get ready for giggles because you're likely to hear them during this unique study of two rhyming words! Make a copy of page 39 for each child. To begin, have students repeat the rhyming words *hat* and *cat,* encouraging them to listen carefully to the similar endings. Then ask students whether cats wear hats. When the giggles subside, ask them what a cat's hat might look like. Take several suggestions. Next, invite a group of students to your art table. Give each child a copy of page 39. After reading the poem aloud, encourage each student to color his cat as desired. Then have him design a hat for his cat by gluing construction paper scraps and other craft materials above the cat's head.

Pairs of Pawprints

No doubt youngsters will be "paws-itively" delighted when they match rhyming picture cards! Cut out the cards on page 37 and scatter them on the floor in a traffic-free area of the room. Invite a group of up to three children to the area. Have a child choose a pawprint, say the name of the picture, and then find the corresponding pawprint to make a rhyming pair. Instruct him to place the cards together. Continue in the same way with each child in the group until all the cards have been matched. Look at all of those kitty prints!

W

Rhy
nelboa
Use a
on the
resem
your fl

To
board
pairs
wheth
answe
cutout
whiske

Sugge
meow

TEC61327

TEC61327

TEC61327

TEC61327

TEC61327

TEC61327

TEC61327

TEC61327

TEC61327

TEC61327

TEC61327

TEC61327

Where Are the Whiskers?

Rhyming words are the cat's meow with this flannelboard activity! Make a cat head cutout from felt. Use a black permanent marker to draw facial features on the cat; then cut six thin strips of black felt so they resemble whiskers. Place the cat head cutout on your flannelboard.

To begin, gather youngsters around the flannelboard. Say a pair of words (use one of the suggested pairs shown if desired). Help youngsters identify whether the words rhyme. After arriving at the correct answer, invite a child to add a whisker to the cat cutout. Continue in the same way until the cat has six whiskers. What an adorable kitty!

Suggested pairs of words: *cat/sat, purr/fur, pet/ meow, fish/wish, paw/claw, mice/dog*

Finicky Felines

Finicky kittens only have an appetite for fish that show rhyming pairs! Make a blue construction paper copy of the fish cards on page 40. Laminate the cards if desired; then cut them out. Locate a plastic bowl to represent a cat's dish. To begin, explain to a small group of children that they are going to pretend to be kittens. Then tell them that they want to have fish for dinner, but they are very picky and will only eat pairs of fish that have rhyming pictures. Place in front of the youngsters three fish, two of which are a rhyming pair. Prompt the students to say the name of the picture on each fish; then help them find the picture whose name does not rhyme with the others. Have the students place the rhyming fish in the food dish. Place the other fish in a separate pile. Continue in the same way for the remaining fish. Time for dinner!

Cat and Hat

What kind of hat
Do you give to a cat?
Would you choose one with
    pictures of mice
Or maybe some fish
Or some milk in a dish?
Yes, a cat would think that's
    rather nice!

Note to the teacher: Use with "A Hat for a Cat" on page 35.

Fish Cards

Use with "Finicky Felines" on page 36.

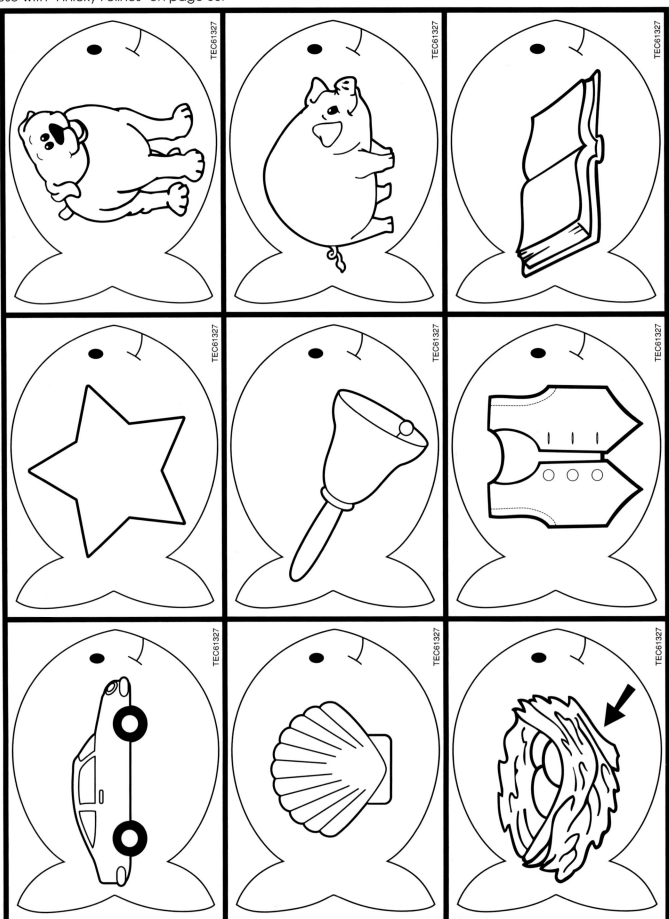

Fun With Phonological Awareness

Little ones will have a ball with these engaging phonological awareness activities!

A Name Song
Rhyming

Here's a toe-tapping song that's sure to get little ones giggling! Lead students in singing the song shown, substituting a nonsense word that rhymes with a student's name and revealing the child's real name in the third line. Prompt the corresponding child to stand at the end of the song and then sit back down. Sing several rounds of this fun tune!

(sung to the tune of "If You're Happy and You Know It")

If your name rhymes with [telly], please stand up! (clap, clap)
If your name rhymes with [telly], please stand up! (clap, clap)
If your name rhymes with [telly], then you surely must be [Kelly].
If your name rhymes with [telly], please stand up! (clap, clap)

Amy Aloi
Bollman Bridge RECC
Jessup, MD

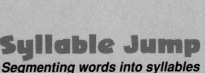

Di-no-saur!

Syllable Jump
Segmenting words into syllables

Collect a variety of objects from your classroom and place them in a container. Gather youngsters around the container. Then have a child remove an object and say its name. Prompt youngsters to stand up and repeat the name as they jump once for each word part. Then have students sit back down. Continue in the same way for each object in the container.

Crazy Zoo Critters
Manipulating phonemes

This sound substitution activity is wildly fun! Remove the ready-to-go cards on page 43 and cut them apart. To begin, hold up the lion card and prompt youngsters to chant the first two lines of the rhyme below. Respond with the final line of the rhyme. Youngsters are sure to correct you, explaining that the animal is called a *lion*, not a *bion*. Then repeat the process with the remaining animal cards, substituting the initial sound in each animal's name.

Children: When you went to the zoo,
           What did you see?
Teacher: I saw a [bion] looking at me!

That's a lion!

A Name Song
Isolating beginning sounds

This little ditty is sure to be popular with your youngsters. Make a name card for each child. Then hold up a card and have students identify the name and corresponding classmate. Finally, lead students in singing the song shown, substituting the appropriate name and initial sound.

(sung to the tune of "The Muffin Man")

[Tammy]'s name begins with [/t/],
Begins with [/t/], begins with [/t/].
[Tammy]'s name begins with [/t/].
[/t/, /t/, /t/, /t/, /t/].

Mary Robles
Little Acorns Preschool
Milwaukie, OR

Dog, frog!

Two Terrific Words!
Rhyming

Spotlight rhyming pairs with this game. Remove the ready-to-go cards on page 45; then cut them apart and place them faceup on a tabletop. Help a child choose two cards with pictures that have rhyming names. Display the cards and then lead students in singing the song shown. Repeat the process with the remaining cards.

(sung to the tune of "London Bridge")

[*Dog* and *frog*] are rhyming words,
Rhyming words, rhyming words.
[*Dog* and *frog*] are rhyming words.
Say them with me!
[Dog, frog]!

Amy Countiss, Washington/Jackson Elementary, Wichita Falls, TX

Wiggle With Beginning Sounds!

Youngsters dig these ideas, which focus on beginning consonant sounds!

ideas by Roxanne LaBell Dearman, Western NC Early Intervention Program for Children Who Are Deaf and Hard of Hearing, Charlotte, NC

Wiggle Worms
Recognizing beginning consonant sounds

Youngsters wiggle their way through sound-matching skills with this energetic song. Have students stand, and teach them the song below. After each verse is sung, hold up two objects or picture cards and say each item's name (make sure you share at least one item or picture that begins with the song's featured letter sound). When youngsters hear an item that begins with the sound sung in the song, have your little worms wiggle down to the ground. Repeat the song several times, substituting the sounds in line 3 to match sounds with which your class is familiar. Wiggle, wiggle!

(sung to the tune of "The Farmer in the Dell")

The earthworm hears a sound.
The earthworm hears a sound.
The earthworm hears a [/p/, /p/, /p/]
Then wiggles in the ground!

Earthworms on the Hunt
Identifying beginning sounds

Little ones dig this hunt in mud when their fingers (worms) search for pictures with the same beginning sounds! To prepare, attach three or four stickers that begin with the same letter—such as ball, bird, and bell stickers—to the inside of a resealable plastic bag. Seal the bag and place it inside a larger resealable plastic bag. Pour half a cup of brown paint into the outer bag to represent mud. Seal the bag and then use clear packing tape to secure the bag's opening. Make several more mud bags to reinforce the sounds that you would like students to practice. Have each child choose a bag, lay it on a table, and then use her little worms to search for pictures in the mud. Encourage each child to determine which sound is heard at the beginning of each picture's name. Have youngsters repeat the activity with a different mud bag. We dig it!

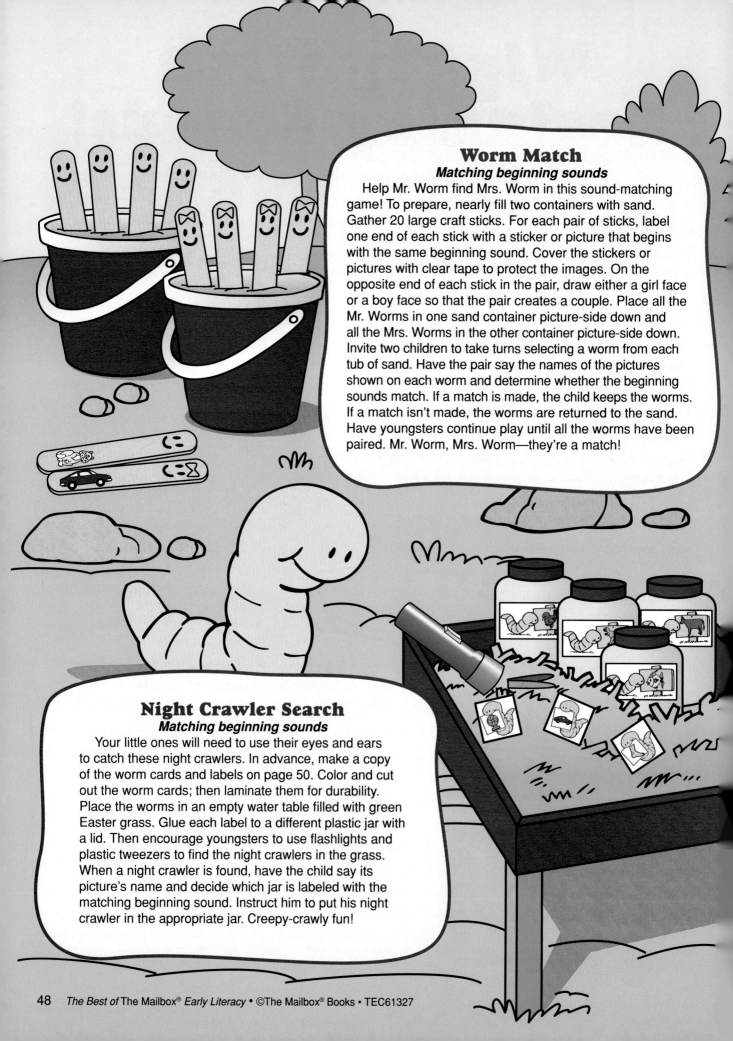

Worm Match
Matching beginning sounds

Help Mr. Worm find Mrs. Worm in this sound-matching game! To prepare, nearly fill two containers with sand. Gather 20 large craft sticks. For each pair of sticks, label one end of each stick with a sticker or picture that begins with the same beginning sound. Cover the stickers or pictures with clear tape to protect the images. On the opposite end of each stick in the pair, draw either a girl face or a boy face so that the pair creates a couple. Place all the Mr. Worms in one sand container picture-side down and all the Mrs. Worms in the other container picture-side down. Invite two children to take turns selecting a worm from each tub of sand. Have the pair say the names of the pictures shown on each worm and determine whether the beginning sounds match. If a match is made, the child keeps the worms. If a match isn't made, the worms are returned to the sand. Have youngsters continue play until all the worms have been paired. Mr. Worm, Mrs. Worm—they're a match!

Night Crawler Search
Matching beginning sounds

Your little ones will need to use their eyes and ears to catch these night crawlers. In advance, make a copy of the worm cards and labels on page 50. Color and cut out the worm cards; then laminate them for durability. Place the worms in an empty water table filled with green Easter grass. Glue each label to a different plastic jar with a lid. Then encourage youngsters to use flashlights and plastic tweezers to find the night crawlers in the grass. When a night crawler is found, have the child say its picture's name and decide which jar is labeled with the matching beginning sound. Instruct him to put his night crawler in the appropriate jar. Creepy-crawly fun!

Walk the Worm
Identifying beginning sounds, pronouncing sounds

Wee learners get lots of practice making consonant sounds as they walk along this winding worm! In advance, attach strips of masking tape to the floor to make a long twisting worm. Place several objects at one end of the worm. Invite a small group of children to join you at the worm. Select one child to be the worm walker. Have her choose an object, name it, and then say its beginning sound. Next, instruct her to walk on the worm while repeatedly saying her featured beginning sound. Encourage the rest of the group to say the sound along with her. Continue play until each child has walked the worm. That's /t/, /t/, /t/, terrific!

Juicy Worms
Matching beginning sounds

What's worse than finding a worm in your apple? Finding half a worm in your apple! Students search for the other half of the worm during this activity. Cut out the worm cards on page 51; then cut each worm in half as shown. Place one half of each worm in an empty, clean apple juice can and place the corresponding halves faceup on a table. Gather a small group of children at the table. Invite a child to choose a worm half from the can. Have the group say the name of the picture on the worm. Then encourage students to find the worm half whose picture begins with the same sound. When the match is found, have the child position the halves to form a whole worm. Continue play until all the worms are put together. Place the worm halves at a center for more practice. What wormy learning fun!

Worm Cards and Labels

Use with "Night Crawler Search" on page 48.

TEC61327
TEC61327
TEC61327
TEC61327
TEC61327
TEC61327
TEC61327
TEC61327
TEC61327
TEC61327
TEC61327
TEC61327
TEC61327
TEC61327
TEC61327
TEC61327

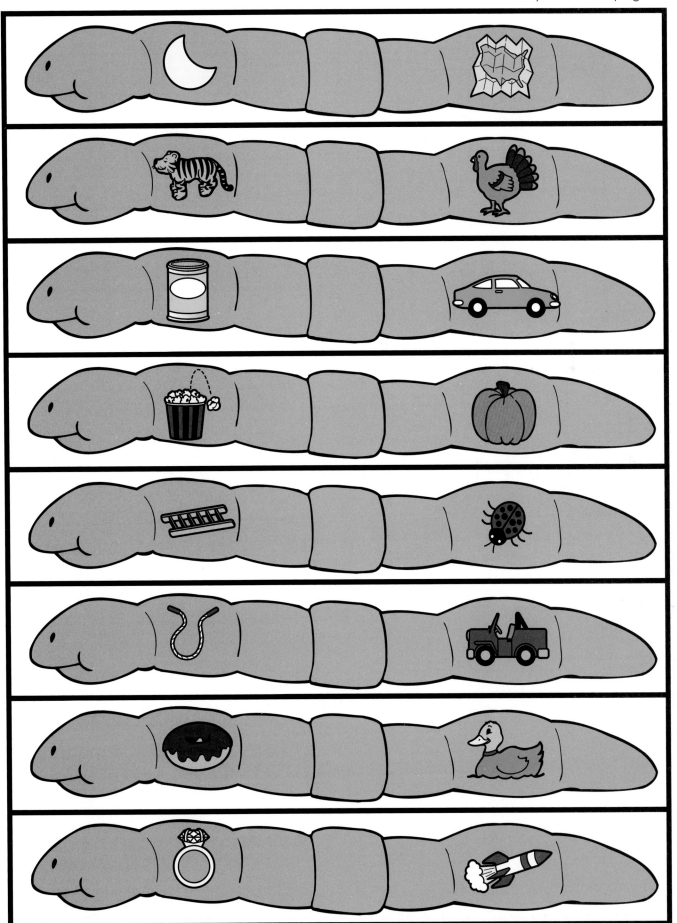

Let's Play With Sounds!

Hearing click-clacking claws and curious growls? No worries—it's just these adorable monsters here to help little ones build phonological awareness skills!

ideas contributed by Lucia Kemp Henry, Fallon, NV

What's to Eat?
Manipulating phonemes

To prepare for this whole-group activity, cut pictures of food from magazines. Also cut out several colorful copies of the monster pattern on page 56. Place the monsters on your floor in a row and place the food cutouts nearby. Have students sit in a circle around the cutouts. Tell youngsters that the monsters are very hungry; then name the food a particular monster wants, changing the initial sound in the food name. For example, you might say, "The green monster would like to have some 'dananas.'" Have youngsters identify the food that the monster wants; then encourage a child to place the appropriate cutout on the monster. Continue in the same way with the remaining food items.

Cute Suit
Reciting a rhyming poem

Give each child a copy of page 56. Lead students in reciting the provided poem several times, prompting them to supply the final word in each rhyming couplet. Next, provide access to crayons, tissue paper squares, and a bowl of glue with paintbrushes. Have little ones use the supplies to give their monsters cute furry suits!

Little Monster looks so cute
In his fuzzy, furry suit.
Should his fur be long and green?
Messy? Curly? Short and clean?
Should his fur be pink and blue?
What does he look like to you?

Odd Monster Out
Identifying nonrhyming words
One little monster in this cuddly trio has to go! Cut out the cards on page 57 and eight colorful copies of the monster on page 56; then lightly tape a different card to each monster. Gather a small group of youngsters and present three monsters, making sure that two of the monsters show pictures whose names rhyme. Lead students in reciting the chant shown. Then help students identify the picture whose name doesn't rhyme with the remaining two. When the monster is identified, have a youngster remove it from the group. Continue in the same way with other monster combinations.

Three little monsters standing in a row.
Two can stay, but one must go!

How Many Words?
Segmenting a sentence into words
Gather a small group of youngsters. Give each child a napkin with Bugles corn snacks (teeth) and a monster face cutout similar to the one shown. Say a simple sentence, such as "The monster is furry." Repeat the sentence and pause after each word, encouraging the child to place one tooth on his monster for each word he hears. When the students are finished, have them count the teeth on their monsters. After several rounds of this activity, have little ones nibble on their snacks!

Beginning and End
Combining segmented words
Cut out two copies of the monster pattern on page 56; then mount each one on a paint stirrer to make stick puppets. Hold one puppet in each hand. Then introduce the monster on your right as "Beginning" and the monster on your left as "End." Explain that Beginning only knows how to say the beginning of words and End only knows how to say the end of words. Tell students that it's very difficult to understand what they are saying and you could use their help. Have Beginning say "pre" and End say "school;" then prompt students to put the fragments together to say the word *preschool*. Continue in the same way with other common words, such as *pumpkin*, *carpet*, *monster*, *footprint*, and *candy*.

A Monster Melody
Singing a rhyming song

Little ones are sure to be delighted with this toe-tapping song. Lead students in singing the song, beginning by singing the chorus and then repeating the chorus again between each verse. Encourage youngsters to sing the rhyming words with extra gusto and to add actions to the performance by stomping their feet, displaying their pointy claws, and showing their gorgeous green teeth!

(sung to the tune of "Alouette")

Chorus
I'm a monster. I'm a silly monster.
I'm a monster. I'm sure you'll agree.

Verses
I can stomp my hairy feet,
Scaring people that I meet.
Hairy feet, that I meet,
Oh!

I can wave my pointy claws.
You will see them on my paws.
Pointy claws, on my paws,
Oh!

My teeth are the color green.
I am sure they're nice and clean.
Color green, nice and clean,
Oh!

Sandy Rothstein
On Our Way Learning Center
Far Rockaway, NY

Cluttered Cave
Identifying rhyming pairs

This monster saves a lot of things inside its cave! In advance, color and cut out a copy of page 56. Also cut out the cards on page 57. Trim a small box so it resembles a cave. Set the monster aside and place the cards inside the cave. After gathering a small group of youngsters around the cave, lead them in reciting the rhyme shown. Have a child peek in the cave; then help him quietly remove two cards with rhyming names. As you repeat the process with each remaining child, pause briefly and say with great drama that you hear the monster coming. Prompt youngsters to be extremely quiet as you "walk" the monster cutout in front of the cave and then back to its previous location. When each child has found a rhyming pair, have them quietly place the cards back in the cave.

Little monster likes to save
Many things inside its cave.
While it's gone, we'll take a peek.
Rhyming words are what we seek.

Monster Pattern

Use with "What's to Eat?" and "Cute Suit" on page 53, "Odd Monster Out" and "Beginning and End" on page 54, and "Cluttered Cave" on page 55.

TEC61327

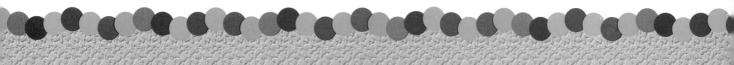

Letters and
Sound Features

A Sweet Selection of Letter Activities

Here's a batch of letter name and sound activities that are just perfect for preschoolers and are frosted with fun!

Freshly Baked Letters

This twist on a familiar chant is a fun way to review letter names! Before reciting the chant, give each child a copy of the cake pattern on page 63 programmed with the first letter of his name. Invite each student, in turn, to name his letter. Encourage one child to hold up his cake. Then lead students in the rhyme shown, inserting the child's letter and name where indicated and encouraging youngsters to pat their legs to the beat of the chant. Continue in the same manner for each remaining child. To complete the activity, invite each youngster to ice his cake by tracing over the letter with colored glue.

Aileen Ellis
Parkview Preschool
Nampa, ID

Patty-cake, patty-cake,
Baker's man!
Bake us a letter
As fast as you can.

Roll it and pat it
And mark it with a [P].
Then put it in the oven
For [Peter] and me!

Name-O

For this small-group game, give each student a supply of O-shaped cereal pieces and a tagboard strip programmed with her name. (Consider grouping students by the number of letters in their names.) Place a set of letter cards in a bag. To play, remove a card and help children announce the letter name. Each child searches her card for a matching letter. If she finds the letter, she covers it with a cereal piece each time it occurs in her name. Play continues until a child covers all her letters and announces, "Name-O!" After verifying her letters, celebrate by inviting all the group members to eat a few pieces of cereal. Then have students clear their cards and play again!

Karen Saner, Burns Elementary, Burns, KS

Search and Circle

Nursery rhymes make this take-home activity extra fun! Choose a nursery rhyme that features a letter youngsters have previously studied. Make a copy of the nursery rhyme, slip it in a large resealable plastic bag, and tape it in place. Place in the bag a letter card and a wipe-off marker. Then give the bag to a child to take home. The child reads the poem with a family member and circles all the letters that match the letter on the card. After she returns the bag and shares her work with you, wipe off the bag and then prepare it for a different student.

Vickie Osborne, Atkins Elementary, Atkins, VA

Marvelous Letter M!

M&M's candy pieces are the inspiration for this taste bud–tempting center! Place at a center the following items: a supersize cookie cutout, a supply of small colorful paper circles, glue, and an ink pad with a letter *M* stamp. When a child visits the center, she stamps an *M* on a small circle while saying, "/m/." Then she glues the resulting candy to the cookie. She continues stamping and gluing as time allows. After each student has had an opportunity to add candy to the cookie, display it for all to see!

Maryann Bennett
North Phoenix Baptist Preschool
Phoenix, AZ

Feed the Dog

These cute canines are hungry for letters! Decorate the underside of a paper plate to create a dog as shown. Staple the rim of the plate to the rim of a second plate, leaving a section open near the dog's mouth. Also staple a paper tongue to the second plate. Make several copies of the bone pattern on page 64 and label each bone with a different letter. Cut out the bones and place them on the floor; then gather youngsters around the bones. Invite a child to choose a bone and hold it up for all to see. Have students name the letter on the bone. Then press the plates inward, as shown, to open the dog's mouth and have the student "feed" the bone to the dog. Play several rounds of this nifty activity!

Bonnie Moore
Lighthouse Christian Academy, Cumberland, MD

The Letter Bus

Youngsters sing letter sounds with this catchy rendition of a familiar song! Enlarge, color, cut out, and laminate a copy of the school bus pattern on page 64. Have a student lightly tape a letter card to the bus; then lead youngsters in singing the song shown. Repeat this rollicking tune several times with different cards!

(sung to the tune of "The Wheels on the Bus")

The [D] on the bus says, "[/d/, /d/, /d/],
[/d/, /d/, /d/, /d/, /d/, /d/]."
The [D] on the bus says, "[/d/, /d/, /d/]"
All the way to school!

Pam Colby
Pam's Puddle Jumpers Family Daycare
Minneapolis, MN

Where Is It?

The search is on with this quick daily activity! Each day before students arrive, remove a letter from your classroom alphabet display and place it somewhere in the room. After all students have arrived for the day, explain, with great drama, that a letter is missing from the alphabet! Help students determine the name of the missing letter. Then invite your young detectives to look around the classroom and locate the letter. When the letter is found, have a student place the letter back where it belongs.

Sally Avila-Garcia, Shepherd of the Valley Preschool and Kindergarten
Hacienda Heights, CA

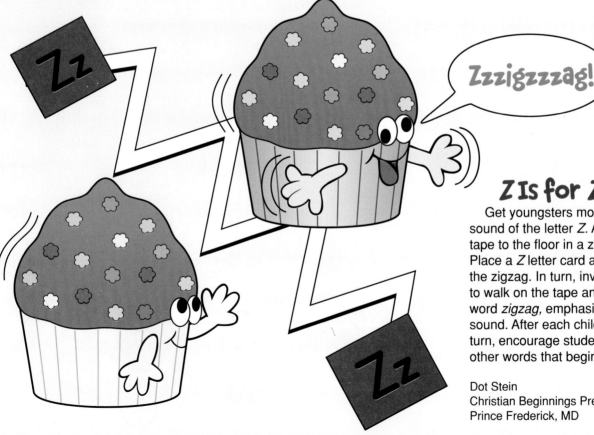

Zzzigzzzag!

Z Is for Zigzag

Get youngsters moving with the sound of the letter *Z*. Attach masking tape to the floor in a zigzag fashion. Place a *Z* letter card at both ends of the zigzag. In turn, invite each child to walk on the tape and repeat the word *zigzag,* emphasizing the /z/ sound. After each child has had a turn, encourage students to name other words that begin with /z/.

Dot Stein
Christian Beginnings Preschool
Prince Frederick, MD

Bone Pattern
Use with "Doggie, Doggie" on page 7 and "Feed the Dog" on page 61.

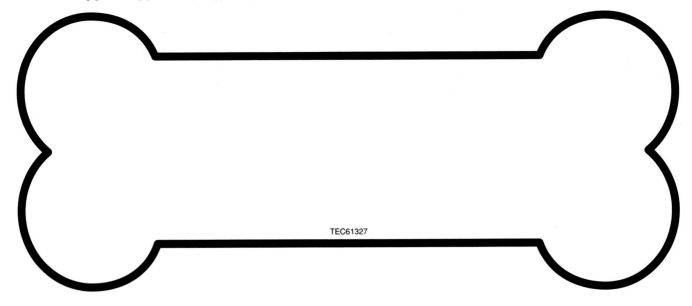

TEC61327

School Bus Pattern
Use with "The Letter Bus" on page 62.

TEC61327

Letters and Sounds

Super Letter Center

Help little ones practice letter recognition and formation at this super center! Obtain a trifold presentation board (or fold cardboard to make a presentation board) and then attach to the board copies of your featured letter and a picture of an animal or object whose name begins with the corresponding letter sound. Place the board at a center along with items such as those shown to help little ones practice forming and recognizing the letter.

Cathy Germino, A Little Folks School House
Manchester, NH

Plunger *O* Placemat

Youngsters are sure to remember the letter *O* with this cute activity! Have youngsters press an unused rubber sink plunger in a pan of paint and then press the plunger on a sheet of paper several times to make a letter *O* placemat. Allow the paint to dry. Then, while students are out of the classroom, place each placemat at the corresponding youngster's seat along with a plate holding a mini doughnut and O-shaped cereal. When students come back to the room, explain that Mr. O came to visit and left special treats in the shape of the letter *O!* Then have little ones nibble on their treats.

Becky Edwards, South Roebuck Baptist Child Development
    Center, Birmingham, AL
Monica Saunders, Hazelwild Farm Educational Center,
    Fredericksburg, VA

Hand Stamps

Place a variety of large letter manipulatives in your group area and gather youngsters around the letters. Sing the song shown, substituting the name of one of the letters on the floor. Choose a child to find the letter. When he does, press a rubber stamp into an ink pad and then stamp his hand. Continue in the same way with each remaining youngster.

(sung to the tune of "The Muffin Man")

When you find the letter [*T*],
The letter [*T*], the letter [*T*].
When you find the letter [*T*],
I will stamp your hand.

Lori Udell, St. John's Weekday School, Wytheville, VA

H Is for Holes

This center activity reinforces the sound of letter *H* and gives youngsters a fine-motor workout as well! Make large construction paper letter *H* cutouts and place them at your center along with several hole punchers. Have youngsters visit the center and punch holes in the letters as they chant, "/h/, /h/, holes."

Dorothy Stein, Christian Beginnings Preschool, Prince Frederick, MD

Sound Suitcase

Use this activity to introduce a letter to your class or to review a letter youngsters have already studied. Gather several items whose names begin with a chosen letter. For example, for the letter *S*, you might choose the items shown. Place the items in a suitcase. To begin, gather youngsters around the suitcase. Explain that the items you have in the suitcase begin with /s/. Have students guess what might be in the suitcase. Then reveal the items with great fanfare.

Missy Goldenberg, Beth Shalom Nursery School, Overland Park, KS

The Sandwich Game

Label each side of a cube-shaped box with a different letter, making sure that three sides are labeled with the letter *S.* Cut craft foam to make two bread slice cutouts and a class supply of sandwich topping cutouts. Place a bread slice on the floor. Have a child roll the cube and identify the letter. If the letter is an *S,* she places one of the toppings on the bread. If the letter is not an *S,* she identifies the letter and then rolls again. Continue until each child has a chance to add a topping. Then place the final slice of bread on the stack of toppings and have youngsters enthusiastically yell, "Sandwich!"

Cross It Out

Give each child a crayon and a clipboard with a sheet of paper labeled with six different letters. Dim the lights slightly, locate one of the letters on materials posted around your room, and then shine a flashlight on the letter. Have students name the letter and then cross out the matching letter on their sheets. Repeat the process for each remaining letter.

Katherine Bryan, T.C.O.C. Head Start, Streator, IL

Choose and Sing

Scatter letter cards in your large-group area. Then gather students around the cards. Encourage a child to choose and name a letter. Lead youngsters in singing the song shown, substituting the child's name, the letter name, and the letter sound where indicated. Have the child place the letter in a separate pile. Then continue in the same way with different youngsters.

(sung to the tune of "He's Got the Whole World in His Hands")

[Sam]'s got the letter [*M*] in his hand.
[Sam]'s got the letter [*M*] in his hand.
[Sam]'s got the letter [*M*] in his hand.
[/m/, /m/, /m/, /m/, /m/, /m/, /m/, /m/].

Cathy Seibel, Greensburg, PA

BCABCABCABCAB

Bear's Belly

What has bear been eating? Why, he's been eating things that begin with /b/! Make a large bear cutout and attach it to a wall. Then cut out the cards on page 69 and place them on a table. Have a child choose a card and then name the picture. Have the remaining students identify whether the name begins with /b/. If it does, help the child attach the card to the bear's tummy. Continue in the same way for each remaining card.

Lottie Hart, Miss Kathy's Early Learning Center, Pensacola, FL

A Stolen Letter

Ready letter cutouts for flannelboard use. Then place four letters on your flannelboard. Have youngsters name the letters on the board. Then, while students cover their eyes, remove a letter. Recite the rhyme shown and then have students name the missing letter. Play several rounds of this entertaining game.

> Hocus-pocus, shimmery shoe,
> Which little letter did I take from you?

Alphabet Everywhere!

Have youngsters look at the wordless picture book *Alphabet City* by Stephen T. Johnson. In this book, natural and manmade objects form the letters of the alphabet. Prompt youngsters to notice the letter in each picture. Next, grab your digital camera and take students on a walk outside the school. Invite youngsters to find objects that look like letters, such as two branches of a tree forming the letter *Y*. Take a photograph of each letter found. Then place the photos along with corresponding letter cards in an album.

Melissa Vervinck, Somerset Early Childhood Center, Rochester Hills, MI

ALPHABET CITY

Stephen T. Johnson

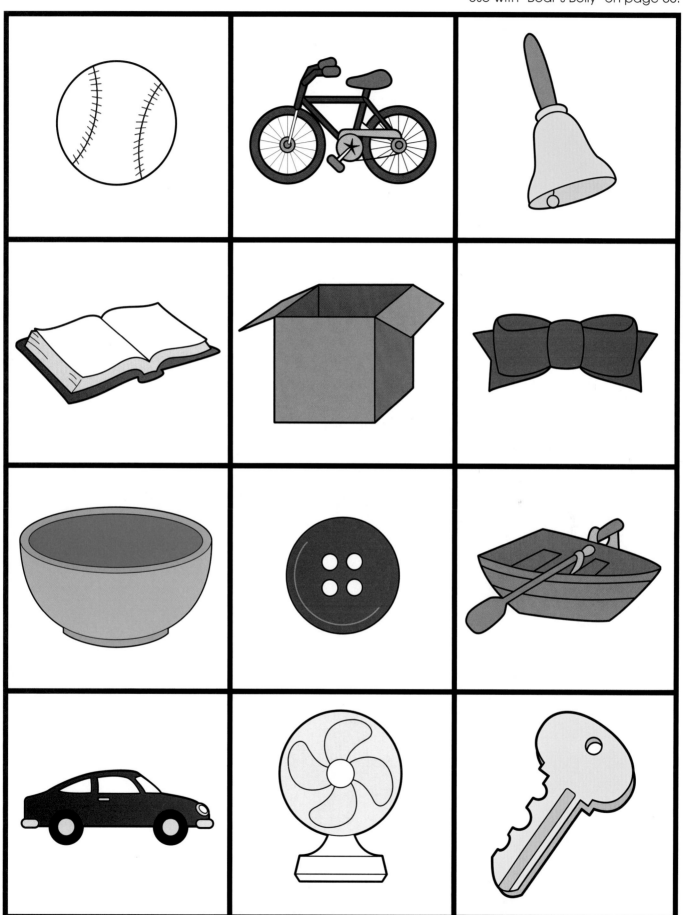

Print Concepts
and
Writing Features

Chugging Into Print Awareness

All aboard for these activities, which help preschoolers understand conventions of print!

by Ada Goren, Winston-Salem, NC

Choo-Choo-Choose a Cover!
Book covers tell about the story inside.

Get this look at books on track by starting at the beginning—a book's cover! Gather students and display three or four books in front of them. Explain that a book's cover and title usually tell the reader something about the story that's inside. Read each book title aloud. Give a short synopsis of one of the stories; then ask whether anyone can identify the book's cover. After a child has correctly identified the cover, talk about how the cover and the story go together. Then move on and give synopses of the other books and have students match those covers too.

Bookmakers
A book is created by an author, an illustrator, and a publisher.

Your preschoolers know that a book's title is on its cover. But what about those names? Hold up a big book and read aloud the author's and illustrator's names, as well as the publisher's name from the title page. Ask whether anyone knows who these people are and why their names are on the book. Explain to students that an author writes a story, an illustrator adds the art, and a publisher is responsible for putting the book together. Then teach youngsters this chant to reinforce these bookmakers' jobs. Invite three children at a time to play the roles of author, illustrator, and publisher. Have them stand in front of the group and point to the appropriate parts of a big book as indicated.

(chanted to Brown Bear, Brown Bear, What Do You See?)

Author, author, what do you do?
I write the words in a book for you.
Point to text.

Illustrator, illustrator, what do you do?
I make the pictures in a book for you.
Point to illustration.

Publisher, publisher, what do you do?
I put the book together for you!
Close book and point to cover.

Cover to Cover
Hold and handle books properly.

Here's an activity engineered to help preschoolers practice handling books correctly and with care! For each child, affix a small sticky note to the front cover of a book. Draw on the sticky note an arrow that points upward. Give each child a book and then ask her to hold the book so that she can see the arrow pointing up. Sing the song at right as youngsters follow along!

(sung to the tune of "The Farmer in the Dell")

The cover goes on top; the cover goes on top.
Hold your book in your lap so the cover goes on top.

Turn one at a time; turn one at a time.
Turn the pages in your book one at a time.

Turn front to back; turn front to back.
Turn the pages in your book from front to back.

Treat your book with care; treat your book with care.
Whenever you read a book, treat that book with care!

Green Means "Go," Red Means "Stop"
Print flows top to bottom and left to right.

Train your little ones to recognize the starting points for reading with some colorful cues! On several green sticky dots, write the word *go*. On several red dots, write the word *stop*. Place each dot on a small sticky note. Choose a page in a big book and display it in front of your group. Point to the top of the page and the bottom of the page. Ask a child to tell you which place you should start reading. Have him place a "go" note at the top of the page. Then ask where to stop reading this page. Have another volunteer put a "stop" note at the bottom of the page. Next, do the same thing with each line of print on the page. Have youngsters mark the left side of each line with green sticky dots and the right side with red ones. Finally, read the page aloud to your group, running your hand under the print to demonstrate the correct starting and stopping points and to emphasize the return sweep at the end of each line.

Story Trains
A story has a beginning, a middle, and an end.

It's full steam ahead when your preschoolers explore the basic parts of a story! Make one copy of the train patterns on pages 74 and 75; then color them. After sharing a story with your students, explain that each story is like a train on a track. Display the engine pattern for the group and write in the title of the book. Then display the train car marked "Beginning." Ask student volunteers to recall what happened at the beginning of the book; then write their dictation on the car. Continue in the same manner with the other boxcar and the caboose. Then review all the parts and remind students that every story has a beginning, a middle, and an end. If desired, repeat the activity on another day with a different story and another set of train car patterns.

Engine and Train Car Patterns
Use with "Story Trains" on page 73.

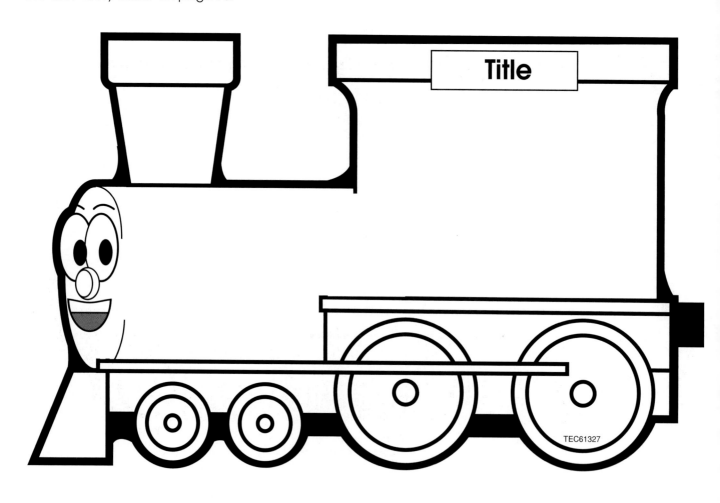

Title

TEC61327

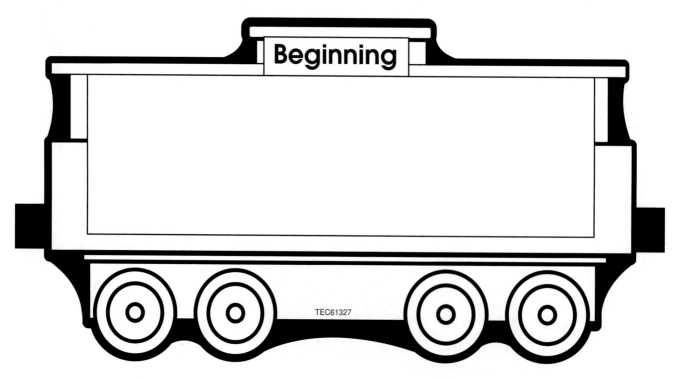

Beginning

TEC61327

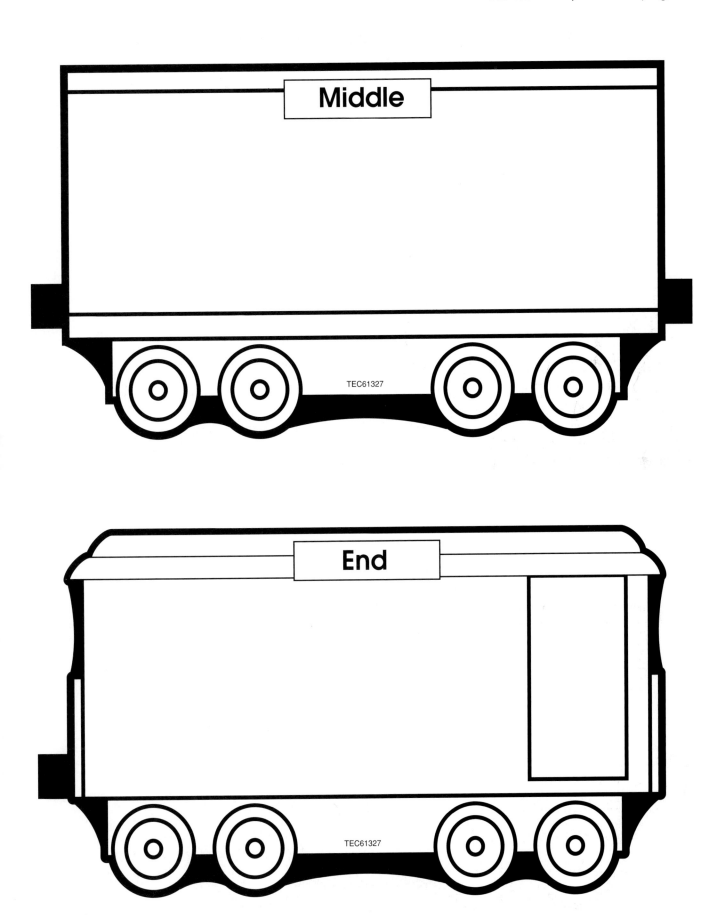

TEC61327

TEC61327

A Cozy Collection of Writing Ideas

Here's a selection of activities to help little ones warm up to writing! With helpful tips, ideas on dictated writing, and ways to zip up your writing center, there are sure to be several ideas just perfect for your little authors.

Daily News

Youngsters dictate information to add to your classroom's daily news! During center time, call a student over to a table and ask him if he has any news he would like to share. As the child shares any desired information, write his words on a sheet of chart paper. Continue in the same way with other youngsters. Then, later in the day, read aloud the daily news to the class. Repeat the activity several times each month, calling on different youngsters to share their news each time.

Sharon K. Swenson
Hazel Lake Montessori
Staples, MN

Daily News

Mom and I are going to the store today.
                            Juan

I like my cat.
                            Ella

I saw Grandma this morning.
                            Lee

I had pancakes for breakfast!
                            Jordan

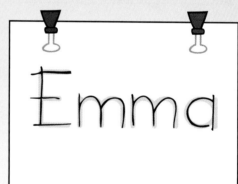

Name-Writing Success!

When little ones are ready to practice writing their names, this tip will help them succeed! Use an extra thick black marker to write each child's name on a separate sheet of copy paper; then laminate the papers for durability. Help a child clip a blank sheet of copy paper on top of the laminated sheet. Her name will show through the paper and she can easily trace it with a marker or chubby crayon. Ah, success!

Beth Lemke, Highland Headstart, Coon Rapids, MN

Super Center Additions

Spice up your writing center by incorporating one or more of the suggestions below. You may wish to rotate center additions to keep interest level high.

- Little ones can roam and write with the addition of clipboards to your writing center! Use a string to attach a writing utensil to each of several clipboards. Then clip a piece of paper to each board. A youngster can roam around the room, writing letters or words he sees!

- Laminate several pieces of environmental print and place them at the center along with dry-erase markers. Youngsters can use the markers to trace letters on the labels, or they can use other available writing utensils to write familiar favorites on provided paper.

- Flash card sets come in many different themes, such as animals, shapes, letters, and colors. Place different sets of flash cards at your writing center on a rotating basis. If desired, you can also use die-cuts to make unique sets of flash cards. Youngsters will enjoy flipping through the cards as well as attempting to write the words they see.

Amber Baker, Learn a Lot Christian Preschool, Moorseville, IN; Monica Grimm, Wasatch Presbyterian Preschool, Salt Lake City, UT; Twilla Lamm, Jenks, OK; Lynne Lenchak, Avon, OH

Here's a quick tip! If youngsters have a difficult time gripping pencils or crayons, invite them to write with a short piece of chubby crayon. Little fingers can't help but grip these the correct way and children often transfer that hold to other writing utensils!

Jennifer Cochran, Morgan County Primary School, Madison, GA

[Santa] , [Santa] , works all day to pack his big red Christmas [sleigh] .

[Santa] , [Santa] , with his [children] , empties toys from all his shelves.

[Santa] , [Santa] , dressed in red, waits for all to go to [bed] .

[Santa] , [Santa] , gives out toys to all the little [girls] and [boys] .

Writing and Rebus Poems

In advance, use the picture cards on page 79 to make a rebus poem poster similar to the one shown. Encourage youngsters to help you chant the poem as you follow the words with your finger. Next, place copies of the picture cards on page 79 at a table along with large pieces of paper and crayons. Invite students to use the pictures to make their own writing. What a fun way to be successful at writing!

Kimberly Corzine, Learning Tree East, Elgin, IL
Louise Frankel, Family Development Day Care, Plainfield, NJ

Splendid Speech Bubbles

To prepare, cut pictures of people from magazines, making sure you have at least one for each child. Also cut out a speech bubble for each youngster. Invite him to choose a picture and decide what that person might say. Write his words on a speech bubble; then encourage him to glue it to a sheet of construction paper along with the corresponding magazine picture. If desired, place additional speech bubbles and magazine pictures at your writing center for continued practice.

Renee Parker, Selinsgrove Area School, Selinsgrove, PA

Sign In!

A center sign-in sheet is an appealing way to have youngsters practice writing their names! In advance, set up an engaging center for youngsters to visit, such as a mock fireside reading area. Then place a clipboard with a sign-in sheet near the center. Tell students that they have to sign in before they can visit the center. This handy little sheet encourages youngsters to visit the area and helps them practice writing their names.

Ella Stroupe
Williams Trace Children's Day Out
Sugar Land, TX

Ladder Stories

In advance, draw a simple picture on a sheet of paper, such as the one shown. Then write the first line of a story underneath the drawing. Gather a small group of youngsters and read aloud the story starter. Ask a student what might happen next. Write the student's words on a sentence strip and then personalize the strip. Continue in the same way, having each remaining youngster contribute a sentence to the story. Then attach the picture and strips to a sheet of chart paper and display it in the room.

Karen Abel
Immaculate Conception School
Spotswood, NJ

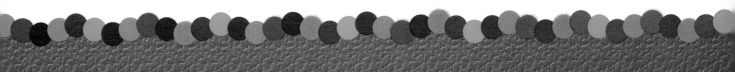

More Literacy Features

Celebrate Literacy
With
Nursery Rhymes!

Little Boy Blue

Odd Animal Options
Understanding that print carries a message

Place word cards for the first few lines of the nursery rhyme in your pocket chart, as shown. Then cut out the cards on page 85 and place them in a bag. Read the words in the chart and then have a child remove a card from the bag. Replace the word *sheep's* with the picture card. Then repeat the process for the word *cow's*. Lead youngsters in reciting the new rhyme. Then continue in the same way with different picture cards.

Little	Boy	Blue,	come	blow	your	horn.
The			in	the	meadow.	
The			in	the	corn.	

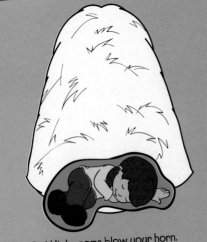

Little Girl Misty, come blow your horn.
The sheep's in the meadow; the cow's in the corn.
Where is the girl who looks after the sheep?
She's under the haystack, fast asleep.

Fast Asleep
Developing an interest in books, writing one's name

Take a photograph of each youngster laying down, pretending to sleep. Cut out her photo and have her glue it to a haystack cutout (see page 87). Then encourage her to glue the haystack to a sheet of construction paper that has been programmed, as shown, for a girl or boy. Have each child write her name in the blank. Then bind the pages together to create a fun class book!

H Is for Hay
Identifying beginning sound /h/

Label a large haystack cutout with the word *hay* and attach it to a wall. Encourage youngsters to name words that begin with the /h/ sound as you write each word on a yellow construction paper strip and then attach the strip to the haystack.

Sing a song of sixpence,
A pocket full of rye,
Four and twenty <u>dinosaurs</u>
Baked in a pie.

Surprise Pie!
Dictating information

Have each child glue a strip of aluminum foil (pie tin) to a sheet of construction paper programmed as shown. Then have her glue a brown construction paper copy of the pie top from page 88 above the tin to make a flap. Encourage her to dictate what she would like to come out of her pie. Write her words in the blank and then have her flip up the pie top and draw an appropriate picture.

Janet Boyce, Cokato, MN

Act It Out!
Speaking to play a game

Encourage students to pretend to be blackbirds as they sit closely in a group. Place a brown blanket (pie crust) over the youngsters as you lead students in reciting the rhyme. When you reach the line "When the pie was opened," whisk off the blanket and encourage students to twitter as if they were blackbirds. Then lead them in finishing the rhyme. Youngsters will be eager to recite this rhyme again and again!

Mini Blackbird Pies
Listening to follow directions

To make a pie, a child crushes two vanilla wafer cookies in a resealable plastic bag. She pours half the crumbs into a foil cupcake liner (pie tin). She mixes mini chocolate chips (blackbirds) with a dollop of vanilla pie filling. Then she pours the mixture over the crumbs and sprinkles the remaining crumbs over the pie filling. That's one tasty blackbird pie!

Janet Boyce

Word Bricks
Developing print awareness

Post a sheet of chart paper on which you've written the rhyme "Humpty Dumpty" and drawn a simple character, as shown. Lead students in reciting the rhyme. Tell students they can see where words begin and end because there are spaces between the words. Then give a child a red marker and help him draw a rectangle around the first word in the rhyme so the rectangle resembles a brick. Continue in the same way with each remaining word. Finally, have youngsters count the number of bricks in Humpty's wall.

Janet Boyce, Cokato, MN

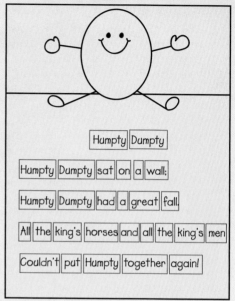

Humpty Dumpty

Humpty Dumpty sat on a wall;
Humpty Dumpty had a great fall.
All the king's horses and all the king's men
Couldn't put Humpty together again!

Charlie

Humpty Dumpty was an egg, and he fell down and got hurt. People tried to help him but they couldn't, so he had to stay broken.

An "Egg-cellent" Summary
Summarizing a story

Have each child draw a face on an egg-shaped piece of clear Con-Tact covering. Then remove the backing and lightly tape the Con-Tact covering, sticky-side up, to a table. Have her tear pieces of facial tissue and stick them on the egg until it is covered. Next, ask her to tell you what happens to Humpty Dumpty as you write her words on a red construction paper wall. Display the finished projects as shown.

Humpty Who?
Rhyming

Display a Humpty Dumpty character on your wall. Prompt youngsters to brainstorm new last names for Humpty, making sure the suggestions always rhyme with its first name. Write each child's suggestion on the cutout. Finally, lead youngsters in reciting the rhyme several times, using one of Humpty's new last names each time. Humpty "Bumpty" sat on a wall!

TEC61327

Pie Pattern
Use with "Surprise Pie!" on page 83.

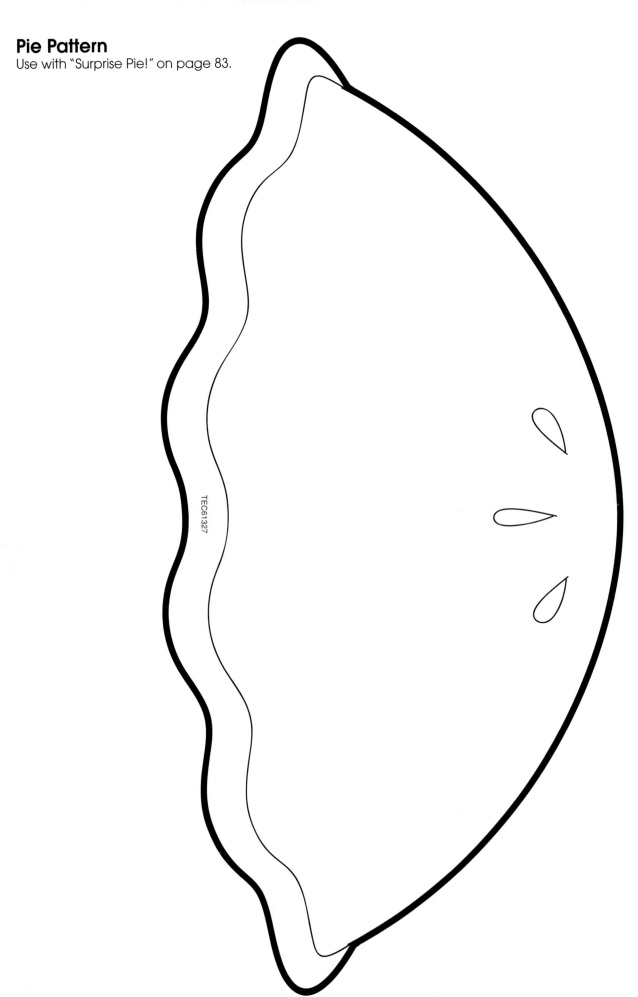

TEC61327

That's My Name!

What better way to begin the school year than with engaging activities that help little ones learn about their written names!

Living Letters

Youngsters are sure to remember this unique letter formation activity. Fill a resealable plastic bag with potting soil and then moisten the soil to make mud. After writing the first letter of each child's name on a separate sheet of cardboard, have him trace his letter with his finger. Then snip a corner from the bag and have the child pipe the mud onto the letter. Encourage him to sprinkle grass seed over the mud. Then place the project near a sunny window. If the mud gets dry, lightly mist the letters. Within a few days, youngsters will see living letters!

Bobbi Chapman
Fiddlesticks Co-op Preschool
Centralia, WA

Make a Match

Use a permanent marker to write each child's name on a separate piece of craft foam. Also write each letter and punctuation mark of each child's name on an individual clothespin. Then store each name with its corresponding clothespins in a separate resealable plastic bag and place the bags at a center. A child finds her name and attaches each clothespin to the corresponding letter. After youngsters have plenty of practice with their own names, encourage them to match clothespins to classmates' names as well.

Patti Ferrick
Child Advocates of Blair County Head Start
Altoona, PA

Seasonal Names

Give each youngster a sheet of construction paper programmed with her name. Then give her two or three markers in colors that correspond to the season. For example, in September you might use fall-related colors and in February you might give her pink and red. Then have her trace over her name several times with each color. If desired, have students attach seasonal stickers around their names. Encourage students to complete a seasonal tracing each month!

Suzanne Maxymuk
Evergreen School
Woodbury, NJ

Letter Hunt

Write the first letter of each child's name on a separate card and place the cards in your pocket chart. Gather student name cards. Hold up a name card and sing the song below, substituting the letter in the song with the first letter in the name. Repeat the song, encouraging youngsters to sing it with you. Then help the youngster whose name you used find her letter card in the pocket chart. Continue in the same way with other name cards.

(sung to the tune of "The Muffin Man")

Have you seen the letter [*G*]?
The letter [*G*], the letter [*G*].
Have you seen the letter [*G*]?
[Grace] needs it for [her] name.

LeeAnn Collins
Sunshine House Preschool
Lansing, MI

Fairy Dust Names

Dip a paintbrush in white glue and give the paintbrush to a child. Wrap your hand around hers and help her use the paintbrush to write her name on a sheet of paper. Have the youngster sprinkle glitter (fairy dust) over the glue. Then help her shake off the excess dust to reveal her name.

Audra Meyerhofer
Long Beach, CA

Preschool Celebrities

This is a fun way to help youngsters practice writing their names while dismissing them for center time! Explain the practice of people asking celebrities for their autographs. Then say, "May I have your autograph, [Lucas]?" and give the youngster a sheet of paper attached to a clipboard. Have the child use a crayon to autograph the paper. Then have the youngster move on to a center.

Carole Watkins
Holy Family Child Care Center
Crown Point, IN

Beginning Sounds

With this simple chant, youngsters hear that their names share beginning sounds with other words. Hold up a student name card and say the youngster's name. Recite a chant, similar to the one shown, two times, substituting the child's name, the name's beginning sound, and a word that shares the beginning sound. As you recite the chant, encourage youngsters to join in and clap along to the beat.

/t/, /t/, /t/,
Tina, Tina, Tina,
/t/, /t/, /t/,
Top, top, top!

Building Names

Use Con-Tact clear covering to attach the letters of each child's name to individual blocks. Place in your block center a book that shows each youngster's photograph and her name. Then encourage each youngster to visit the block center and build her name and her classmates' names.

Kelly Ash
Waukesha County Head Start
Waukesha, WI

Literacy With Little Miss Muffet

ideas contributed by Lucia Kemp Henry
Fallon, NV

Eeeeeeeeeeeeeeeeeeeeeeeeeeeeek!!

Act It Out!

Dramatizing a nursery rhyme

Invite youngsters to pantomime this nursery rhyme with a few simple props! To begin, make the simple headband shown, using pieces of Velcro fastener to make the headband adjustable to any head size. Post the nursery rhyme in your large-group area. After youngsters become familiar with the rhyme, encourage a volunteer to don the headband. Have a second volunteer sit on a footstool (tuffet) with a bowl and spoon. Then, as the remaining youngsters recite the rhyme, prompt the volunteers to act out the words.

Laura Sabin, Educational Child Care
Center, Lansing, MI

M Is for Miss Muffet!

Familiarizing youngsters with letters and sounds

Place several letter *M* cutouts in your sensory table along with a supply of white packing peanuts (curds and whey). Color and cut out a copy of the Miss Muffet pattern on page 94 and place the cutout nearby. Provide several plastic bowls and spoons. A child serves up the curds and whey, removing the *M*s. As he places each *M* on Miss Muffet, he says "/m/."

The Spider Beside Her
Listening

Have each child color and cut out a copy of the spider pattern on page 94. Then have each youngster sit on the floor with her spider in her hand. Help students recite the rhyme "Little Miss Muffet," prompting each child to place her spider beside her when indicated. Repeat the rhyme, substituting different positional words, such as *behind, in front of,* and *on,* encouraging youngsters to position their spiders accordingly.

Haha

HeeHee

HeeHee

Haha

Little Miss Who?
Developing phonological awareness

You're sure to hear lots of giggles when youngsters manipulate phonemes with this activity! Help students name a nonsense word that rhymes with *Muffet,* such as *Duffet, Wuffet,* or *Guffet.* Then lead youngsters in reciting the rhyme, replacing *Muffet* with the new word. Repeat the activity several times with different nonsense words.

Miss Muffet's Meal
Writing

To make a class book cover, color and cut out a copy of the Miss Muffet pattern on page 94. Then attach the cutout to the inside of a paper plate along with the poem shown. Give each child a paper plate and encourage her to draw something Miss Muffet could eat instead of curds and whey. Have her name the food item as you write her words on the plate. Stack the plates under the cover and bind the plates together as desired. Then read the book aloud.

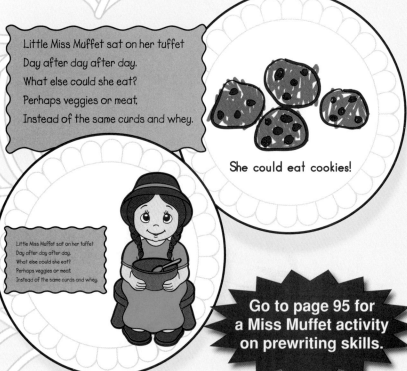

Little Miss Muffet sat on her tuffet
Day after day after day.
What else could she eat?
Perhaps veggies or meat,
Instead of the same curds and whey.

She could eat cookies!

Go to page 95 for a Miss Muffet activity on prewriting skills.

Miss Muffet Pattern
Use with "*M* Is for Miss Muffet!" on page 92 and "Miss Muffet's Meal" on page 93.

Spider Pattern
Use with "The Spider Beside Her" on page 93.

Lots of Spiders!

Note to the teacher: Give a child a copy of this page. Draw a simple spider on a sticky dot and attach it to the top of his index finger. Then have him trace the lines with his finger. If desired, also have him trace the lines with a crayon.

Topic and Skill Index